NATIONAL GEOGRAPHIC

Ladders

THE
INCA
Pre-Columbian Americans

WHO WERE THE INCA?

by Andrea Alter

Mysterious. Brilliant. Powerful. These words describe the Inca. This civilization lived in South America before Columbus came to the Americas. The Inca emerged as a mountain culture in central Peru around the year A.D. 1100. In only a few hundred years, their empire extended 2,500 miles and ruled 12 million people. Their quick rise amazes historians. It might amaze you, too!

Here is where the Inca lived.

You're looking at the Inca ruins of Machu Picchu, which sit at 8,000 feet above sea level in the Andes Mountains. What was this place, and why did the Inca build it? What are those green "steps"? Find out in the pages ahead.

THE EMPIRE BUILDERS

Let's look at where the Inca lived—in the Andes, some of the highest mountains in the world. These mountains extend the length of the western side of South America. Peaks of more than 20,000 feet overlook deep gorges, or steep canyons. This wasn't the easiest place to build a large empire.

The mountainous land didn't discourage the Inca, though. In a short period of time, a series of Inca rulers overpowered neighboring groups to build the empire. At its height, the Inca Empire included parts of present-day Colombia, Ecuador, Peru, Bolivia, Chile, and Argentina.

How did the Inca manage such a large empire? First, Inca society was highly organized, with Inca emperors at the top. Emperors were considered **descendants**, or relatives, of the Inca sun god. Families belonged to larger kinship groups that shared land and worked together. Everyone worked for the empire—whether road building, farming, making pottery, or mining for gold and silver.

To connect distant villages and cities, the Inca built stone roads, trails, and suspension, or rope, bridges that hung over impassable rivers and gorges. Quick communication also strengthened the empire. Runners relayed messages, sometimes covering 140 miles in a day.

The Inca built a powerful empire in only a few hundred years. But would it last?

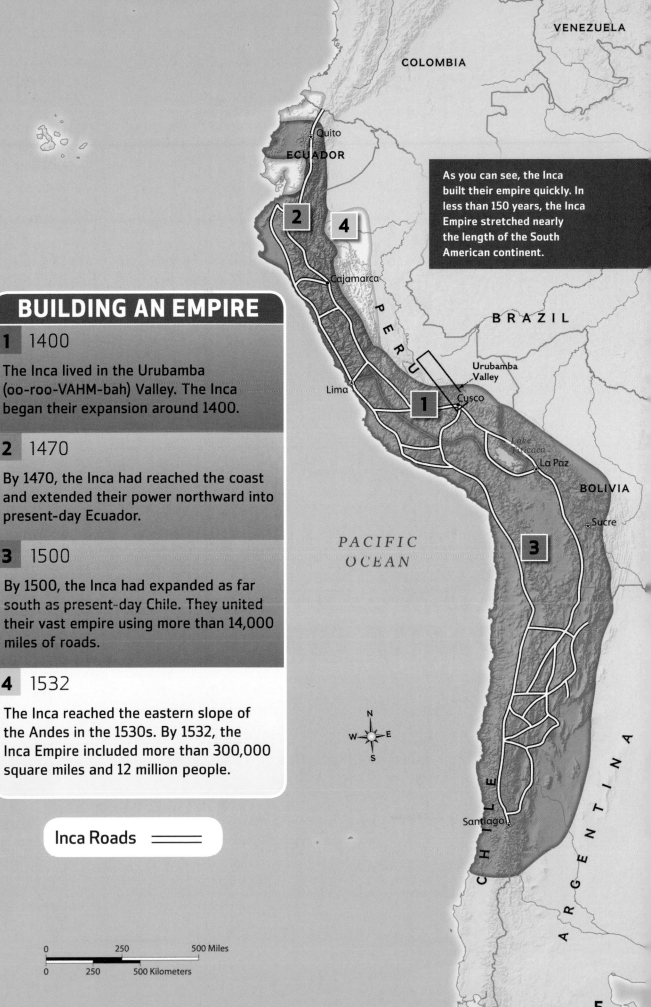

VENEZUELA

COLOMBIA

Quito

ECUADOR

2

4

Cajamarca

As you can see, the Inca built their empire quickly. In less than 150 years, the Inca Empire stretched nearly the length of the South American continent.

P E R U

B R A Z I L

Lima

Urubamba Valley

1

Cusco

Lake Titicaca

La Paz

BOLIVIA

Sucre

PACIFIC OCEAN

3

C H I L E

A R G E N T I N A

Santiago

BUILDING AN EMPIRE

1 1400

The Inca lived in the Urubamba (oo-roo-VAHM-bah) Valley. The Inca began their expansion around 1400.

2 1470

By 1470, the Inca had reached the coast and extended their power northward into present-day Ecuador.

3 1500

By 1500, the Inca had expanded as far south as present-day Chile. They united their vast empire using more than 14,000 miles of roads.

4 1532

The Inca reached the eastern slope of the Andes in the 1530s. By 1532, the Inca Empire included more than 300,000 square miles and 12 million people.

Inca Roads ══════

0   250   500 Miles
0   250   500 Kilometers

N
W   E
S

THE SPANISH CONQUEST

The Inca Empire rose and fell quickly over a period of 132 years. Internal fighting and disease weakened the empire. Then, in the late 1520s, the arrival of Spanish **conquistadors**, or conquerors, spelled disaster for the Inca.

The conquistadors were seeking treasures of gold and silver for the king of Spain. The king appointed conquistador Francisco Pizarro as the governor of Peru and granted Pizarro permission to conquer the Inca. In 1532, Pizarro and a small group of soldiers defeated the Inca and captured their emperor, Atahualpa (ah-tah-WAHL-pah).

The Inca capital, Cusco (KOO-skoh), fell soon after. The Spanish established a new capital at Lima in 1535. The Inca Empire had come to an end.

What happened to the Inca after the Spanish conquest? Inca life and culture changed dramatically. The Inca had to learn the Spanish language. Some Inca fled to high mountains or the jungles of the Amazon Basin. Others stayed and became laborers under Spanish rule.

Inca life changed, but their influence remained. The Inca left behind beautiful artifacts and structures. Later generations were amazed by the skill and brilliance of the Inca.

Since the 1500s, Inca culture has been passed down among the Quechua (KECH-wah). The Quechua are the descendants of the Inca, and are an **indigenous**, or native, people in South America. Most Quechua live in the mountains of Peru, but some live in Bolivia and Ecuador. They maintain their culture through their language, religion, farming, and art.

The language the Quechua speak is also called *Quechua*. Educators in Peru want to increase Quechua language instruction in schools to be sure the Quechua language does not disappear.

Farming techniques have not changed much in this region since the time of the Inca. The Quechua still grow potatoes and other crops on **terraces**, or raised fields cut into the mountainsides. These terraces create flat fields for planting crops, and capture rainwater that would otherwise flow off the mountain slopes.

Like the Inca did, the Quechua raise sheep, llamas, and alpacas for wool. They spin and dye the wool to form vibrant yarns. Skilled Quechua artisans then weave the yarns into blankets, shawls, scarves, bags, and ponchos (PON-chohs). Their weavings often feature animals and plants in traditional designs that connect the Quechua to the Inca culture of the past.

⌃ This Quechua weaver uses a llama bone tool, called a *wichuna,* for choosing and pushing threads into a tightly woven pattern.

> ∧ This Quechua student's uniform reflects his culture's traditional dress. Quechua schoolchildren in Peru learn Quechua and Spanish.

Check In Where and when did the Inca live, and who are their descendants today?

LLAND of the LLAMA

by Sheri Reda

To most people, llamas are curious-looking animals with heavy-lidded eyes and goofy smiles. But llamas were very important to the Inca Empire. The Inca tended huge herds of llamas. They wove images of llamas into cloth and buried their dead with golden llama figurines. The Inca depended on these strong, woolly creatures in many ways.

The Inca lacked wheeled vehicles, but they didn't need them—they had llamas to transport them and their goods around their mountain empire. For example, Inca builders used llamas to carry heavy stones and other building materials over rugged terrain.

Inca farmers used llamas to carry water to their fields. They used llama dung, or waste, as fertilizer for crops and fuel for fires. Llama wool was woven into blankets and cloaks. When a llama died, its fat was used to make candles, its hide was used to make leather, and its meat fed the hardworking Inca. Llamas just might be one of the most useful animals around.

Llamas can live and work in high mountain regions.

Cool Things About Llamas

Can you guess which animal is a close relative of llamas? Camels! Llamas don't have humps, but they are one of four camel relatives that live in South America—the others are alpacas, vicuñas (vih-KOON-yuhz), and guanacos (gwuh-NAH-kohz). Llamas are perfectly suited to live high up in the Andes Mountains. Let's hear more straight from the llama's mouth.

Hello, llama fans! I bet I can guess what you want to ask me. "Do I spit?" Llamas have gotten a bad rap, but we don't spit unless we're mad or threatened. And we don't often get mad at humans. But if we DO, watch out . . .

Some of us wear ear tags for identification. Check out our beautiful, banana-shaped ears. Ear shape is one way to tell us apart from alpacas. They have straight ears. Boring!

My fine, downy undercoat keeps me soft and warm. The wool of my undercoat is so soft and beautiful that people use it to make blankets and clothing.

You only have one stomach? I have three! My three stomachs help me digest grass and shrubs, so I can go long distances without stopping to eat or drink. I can go for days without water, though not as long as my camel cousins in Asia.

My feet are made for mountain climbing. My two big toes help me balance on steep, uneven soil. My soles are tough and leathery to protect my feet from rocky trails. Plus, my hooves are perfectly formed for climbing the rocky Andean mountainsides.

I have coarse guard hair over my undercoat, which protects me from moisture and dirt. It's just an old overcoat, but people love it. I don't mind if folks take some from time to time. I can always grow more.

I am adorable, but I am also supercharged. My blood has more kinds of red blood cells than most other mammals, and these cells help carry oxygen throughout my body. That gives me energy, even high in the mountains where the air doesn't have much oxygen.

Woolly and Warm

When it comes to wool, llamas get a two-for-one deal. Their soft undercoat protects them against extreme cold or heat. Their guard hair repels moisture and dirt, keeping llamas—and people wearing llama wool—comfortable and dry. Llama wool comes in several natural colors, including black, dark brown, reddish brown, white, and gray. And it doesn't shrink in the wash.

To get the wool off a llama, farmers first use wire brushes or leaf blowers to remove dust and dirt from the llama. Then they **shear**, or shave off, the wool, leaving a little behind to keep the llama warm. Most farmers today shear their llamas with electric clippers, but more traditional farmers use a sharp knife. That might sound scary, but this haircut doesn't hurt the llama at all, and the shearer ends up with five to twenty pounds of wool.

A Peruvian woman spins llama wool into yarn.

Leaves, roots, and bug bodies are ground into powder to make dyes. These dyes give llama yarn its brilliant colors.

It takes a few more steps to turn llama wool into a beautiful **textile**. A textile is a piece of cloth or woven fabric. Llama wool can be dyed many colors, including a bright red color made from female cochineal (KAH-chuh-neel) insects. Most dyes are made with natural materials, such as different types of plants.

Craftspeople spin the wool into yarn. Then they knit the yarn into clothing, twist the yarn into rope, or weave it to make cloth or rugs. Artists use it to create beautiful wall hangings, prized around the world. Leave it to a llama to offer usefulness, beauty, and comfort, all at once.

A merchant sells colorful llama yarn at this market in Peru.

Check In   How have llamas adapted to life in the Andes Mountains?

A Tour of Machu Picchu

by Mary Peake

Lace up your hiking boots! It's time to visit one of the world's most fascinating historical sites— Machu Picchu (MAH-choo PEE-choo).

Machu Picchu, which means "old peak," was a small Inca city built in the 1400s. Perched high in the Andes Mountains, Machu Picchu overlooks the Urubamba River Valley, also known as the Sacred Valley. Machu Picchu was built hidden in the mountains, 70 miles from the capital of the Inca Empire. Its **remote** location helped preserve it. For hundreds of years, the world did not know it existed.

To get to Machu Picchu, you could take a train from Cusco, Peru. Or you could hike the 28-mile trail from the Urubamba River up to the historic site. Some people take four days to complete the hike, while others start midway up for a two-day trek.

You have to be in really good shape to hike this trail. At points along the way, you will be 12,000 feet above sea level. When you cross Dead Woman's Pass, you will be at around 13,800 feet!

If you plan to visit Machu Picchu, keep an eye on the weather. The rainy season is between October and April. The dry season between May and September is the most popular with tourists.

> Machu Picchu is nearly 8,000 feet above sea level. The mountain in the background is Wayna Picchu, which means "young peak."

∧ Stones laid by the Inca guide hikers along the Inca Trail. It is one of the most popular hiking trails in South America.

A llama looks over the Central Plaza at Machu Picchu.

Mysterious Mountain City

Let's explore the history of Machu Picchu. This Inca city was built around 1450. The Inca left no written records, so historians and archaeologists—those who study ancient cultures by looking at what the people left behind—came up with theories about why Machu Picchu was built. One theory was that it served a religious function; another was that it was a hiding place for Inca rulers after the Spanish arrived.

Today, archaeologists believe that Machu Picchu was built as a retreat for the emperor Pachacuti (pah-chah-KOO-tee). It was a place where he could "get away" from the demands of his rule. Machu Picchu was abandoned in the early 1500s, before the Spanish conquest. The Spanish destroyed many important sites after conquering the Inca, but Machu Picchu remained intact. Why? The Spanish never found it.

Machu Picchu sat untouched for several hundred years. Then, in 1911, a man named Hiram Bingham was led by a Peruvian guide to jungle-covered walls. He cleared away some of the thick plants that hid the buildings and revealed the true genius of the city. Bingham took thousands of photographs and mapped the site.

Hundreds of archaeologists have studied Machu Picchu since Bingham. They, along with Bingham, have uncovered the advanced techniques the Inca used to build the walls and waterworks. Machu Picchu is truly one of the most interesting places in the world.

Hitting the Highlights

Machu Picchu has two main sections: the Agricultural Section, where the Inca farmed, and the Urban Section, where they lived. The Agricultural Section includes the terraces where the Inca grew crops. It also contains a cemetery, and a guardhouse.

In the Urban Section, the emperor's residence is near the first of a series of fountains. This meant the highest-ranked Inca would have access to the purest water that flowed through the city. The Central Plaza runs through the middle of Machu Picchu. It sits above the section where workers lived and below temples and places where **rituals**, or religious ceremonies, were carried out. The Temple of the Sun and the Royal Tomb are also located in the Urban Section.

Throughout Machu Picchu, the Inca shaped stones without using complex tools. They also did not use mortar, a cement-like material, to hold stones together. Instead, they sculpted each large brick to fit tightly with others. Finally, their buildings had roofs made of grasses and plant materials to keep out sun and rain.

∧ The granite terraces at Machu Picchu were built from the base of the mountain up. Terraces such as these in the Agricultural Section gave the Inca flat spaces to grow crops.

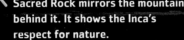
Sacred Rock mirrors the mountain behind it. It shows the Inca's respect for nature.

These stones fit tightly together. Even a piece of paper cannot slide through the cracks between them.

The Inca built the Temple of the Condor onto a natural rock formation that looked like a flying condor. A rock on the floor of the temple represents the condor's head.

Salt Ponds and Circle Terraces

Machu Picchu is fascinating, but the Urubamba Valley is full of many other interesting Inca sites.

The Inca harvested salt at Las Salinas (sah-LEE-nahs). These salt ponds are still in operation today. The Inca built terraces to catch water from a **saline**, or salty, stream. Water from the saline stream above the terraces flows into more than 1,000 small ponds. In the dry season, the water evaporates and workers harvest the salt that remains.

Ollantaytambo (ah-lon-tay-TAHM-boh) is a mountain village high above the Urubamba River. People have been living there since the 1200s. Ollantaytambo served as an Inca **fortress**, or military fort, where the Inca successfully fought off the Spanish during the conquest.

The circle terraces at Moray (mohr-AY) were built in three enormous pits. Temperatures varied significantly from the bottom to the top. This allowed the Inca to experiment with which crops grew best at certain temperatures.

⌃ **The Inca used these circle terraces for farming experiments.**

◀ **Find the people in the photo to get an idea of how large these salt ponds are.**

My Inca Adventure

"It's a breathtaking place!" says Brian Nehlsen. In 2009, he visited the Urubamba Valley and toured Inca sites. Here is his account of the trip.

On the first day, I toured Machu Picchu. I arrived by bus at 5:30 in the morning and took some terrific photographs. The next day I went to Ollantaytambo. I was impressed by the water management system there. A mountain stream flows down into specially built canals—and it is still flowing today. On my third day, I visited Las Salinas and Moray. At Las Salinas, I marveled at how the Inca harvested so much salt from such a tiny stream. I bought some salt candy at the site. At Moray, a short distance from Las Salinas, I walked to the bottom of the terraces. I wondered, "How did the Inca build these nearly perfect circles?" I had a lot of fun in the Urubamba Valley. If I had the chance, I would definitely go back!

Check In   What features of the Inca sites demonstrate Inca skills?

HIGH-ALTITUDE Archaeology

by Andrea Alter

High-altitude **archaeology** has taught us a lot about the Inca. Archaeology is the study of how people lived in the past. High-altitude archaeologists learn about how people lived in high altitudes long ago by studying artifacts they have left behind.

One challenge for high-altitude archaeologists is getting to work. They have to be good hikers—even mountain climbers—to reach their study sites. Some sites are 10,000 to 20,000 feet above sea level, where there is less oxygen. Lack of oxygen can cause people to feel tired and nauseous. So, high-altitude archaeologists must adapt to these conditions and develop the strength of athletes.

Archaeology at high altitudes also includes the risk of avalanches, rockslides, snowstorms, and falls. Winds can be fierce 10,000 feet above sea level, and temperatures can drop suddenly. To stay safe and warm, high-altitude archaeologists must use the right mountaineering gear.

High-altitude archaeologists study different cultures around the world. In the Rocky Mountains of the United States, archaeologist Chris Morgan researches prehistoric settlements. Archaeologist Johan Reinhard works in the mountains of Peru, and Constanza Ceruti works in Argentina. Both of these high-altitude archaeologists work with National Geographic. They study the Inca in South America.

High-altitude archaeologists work in mountain ranges all over the world. The Wind River Range is a mountain range in Wyoming. It stretches along the Continental Divide in the western United States.

Chris Morgan's team sifts excavated material through a screen at a prehistoric village site in Wyoming.

Johan Reinhard Makes a Discovery

Johan Reinhard is not afraid to conquer a mountain. He has made more than 200 treks to high **summits**, or tops of mountains.

Reinhard is a high-altitude archaeologist and a National Geographic Explorer. As a boy, Reinhard liked detective stories and mountain climbing. Now he studies the sacred rituals of mountain people. He began by studying cultures in Nepal. He has since spent three decades learning about mountain people in the Andes.

In 1995, Reinhard and his climbing partner, Miguel Zárate, were hiking on Nevado Ampato (ahm-PAH-toh), a 20,700-foot mountain in Peru. The two noticed something unusual below them. They hiked down to it and made an extraordinary find—a frozen Inca mummy!

> Johan Reinhard has discovered more than 50 Inca ritual sites. Here, Reinhard and his team hike an icy ridge on Nevado Ampato.

JOHAN REINHARD read about explorers when he was a boy and decided to live a life of adventure. Although he is a famous high-altitude archaeologist, his first archaeological job was underwater. He studied Roman shipwrecks in the Mediterranean Sea. In the Andes, Reinhard has gone diving to explore Lake Titicaca, a lake high in the mountains.

Only a few frozen mummies have ever been discovered on high summits in the Andes, and this one was very well preserved. This female mummy had been frozen for hundreds of years. Medical experts used x-rays and chemical analysis to determine her age and health before she died.

Reinhard found gold figurines, cloth bags, and pottery used for burial rituals near the mummy. These artifacts confirmed that Nevado Ampato was a sacred Inca site. Reinhard's discovery helped us learn more about Inca rituals and encouraged him to continue searching high in the Andes.

∧ Sub-zero Andean temperatures preserved the mummy Johan Reinhard and Miguel Zárate discovered.

Constanza Ceruti Fulfills Her Dream

Some people know exactly what they want to be when they grow up. By the age of 14, Constanza Ceruti, a National Geographic Explorer, knew she wanted to be a high-altitude archaeologist. Ceruti grew up in Argentina and now specializes in sacred mountain sites of the Inca. She spends weeks at a time enduring frostbite, blizzards, lightning, and long hikes up and down from basecamp. However, she loves what she does for a living.

The mummies Ceruti discovered are at a museum in Salta, Argentina. They are displayed in refrigerated, low-oxygen cases.

In 1999, Ceruti was working in Argentina at the summit of Mount Llullaillaco (yoo-yay-AH-koh) with Johan Reinhard and his team. At 22,000 feet above sea level, it is the world's highest archaeological site. Conditions on the summit were brutal. It was very cold, and the winds were whipping with great force. The team was excavating Inca ruins, hopeful to find evidence of Inca mountain rituals, when they discovered three mummies!

Leaving the summit, the team had to be sure the mummies stayed frozen. If they thawed, scientists would not be able to study them. The team carried the mummies down the steep mountain quickly and carefully. Once at the base, they placed the mummies in dry ice and took them to a laboratory. After Ceruti and Reinhard studied them, the mummies were put on display at a museum in Argentina.

CONSTANZA CERUTI was born in Argentina. As a high-altitude archaeologist, she has climbed more than 100 mountains higher than 16,500 feet all over the world. She loves to work in the Andes Mountains. There she combines her love of mountain climbing with her enthusiasm for learning more about the Inca.

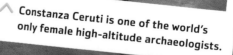

Constanza Ceruti is one of the world's only female high-altitude archaeologists.

Check In   What are some of the main challenges that high-altitude archaeologists face?

Inca Artifacts

by Lily Tucker

When high-altitude archaeologists return from a dig, they often bring back **artifacts**, or items made by humans. Lucky for us, some of these artifacts are displayed in museums. The artifacts help us learn what the Inca valued and how they lived.

The Inca treasured the gold and silver that they mined in the Andes. Spanish conquistadors heard tales of these riches. During and after the conquest, the Spanish **looted**, or stole, these treasures from the Inca and melted them down. Fortunately, some artifacts survived.

> Gold llama, 15th century

< Gold female figurine, 15th century

Many small gold and silver llamas and figurines have been found at Inca burial sites. The figurines wear tiny woven wraps, fastened with a gold or silver pin. Both the ceremonial use of precious metals and the wealth they brought to the Inca and their conquerors show the importance of gold and silver in the Inca Empire.

Some Inca artifacts, such as vessels, or containers, tell us about past rituals. An *aryballos* (ar-uh-BY-yohs) is a vessel that held *chicha* (CHEE-chah), a beverage made from corn. During religious ceremonies, the Inca filled an aryballos with chicha. They poured the chicha on the ground to ask the gods for a good growing season.

< Aryballos, 15th century

> Quipu, 15th century

The Inca used a system of knotted counting cords called *quipus* (KEE-poos) to record information. Quipu means "knot" in Quechua. The placement and colors of knots on quipus helped the Inca count crops, livestock, and weapons. Quipus also kept track of dates and events. Quipus were created and read by trained Inca workers.

Check In   What can we learn about the Inca from the artifacts they left behind?

Discuss

1. What do you think connects the five pieces you read in this book? What makes you think that?

2. How did the Inca build such a powerful and amazing empire? What caused the empire to come to an end?

3. Describe how llamas were important to the Inca and how they are still valued by the Quechua.

4. How have high-altitude archaeologists contributed to our knowledge of the Inca?

5. What do you still wonder about the Inca? What would you like to learn more about?